50 Ramen
Recipes for Home

By: Kelly Johnson

Table of Contents

- Classic Shoyu Ramen
- Miso Ramen with Tofu and Mushrooms
- Spicy Kimchi Ramen
- Vegetarian Ramen with Roasted Vegetables
- Tonkotsu Ramen with Pork Belly
- Vegan Ramen with Seared Tofu
- Chicken Ramen with Soft-Boiled Egg
- Thai Coconut Curry Ramen
- Spicy Pork Ramen with Bok Choy
- Garlic Shrimp Ramen
- Beef Ramen with Stir-Fried Vegetables
- Sesame Soy Ramen with Spinach
- Hawaiian Poke Ramen Bowl
- Szechuan Spicy Ramen
- Smoked Salmon Ramen
- Teriyaki Chicken Ramen
- Creamy Pumpkin Ramen
- Ramen Carbonara
- Lobster Ramen with Miso Broth
- Lemon Ginger Chicken Ramen
- Spicy Tofu Ramen with Sriracha
- Curry Laksa Ramen
- Creamy Mushroom Ramen
- Korean Jjajangmyeon Ramen
- Duck Ramen with Hoisin Sauce
- Thai Peanut Ramen
- Spicy Tuna Ramen
- Pork Ramen with Kimchi and Egg
- Coconut Lime Chicken Ramen
- Japanese Curry Ramen
- Vegetarian Ramen with Crispy Tofu
- Beef Bulgogi Ramen
- Creamy Pesto Ramen
- Mexican Ramen with Black Beans and Avocado
- Lemongrass Chicken Ramen

- Teriyaki Salmon Ramen
- Italian Sausage Ramen
- Vegetable Ramen Stir-Fry
- Chipotle Chicken Ramen
- Shrimp Tempura Ramen
- Moroccan Spiced Lamb Ramen
- Thai Red Curry Ramen
- Vegan Ramen with Shiitake Mushrooms
- Hawaiian Lomi Lomi Salmon Ramen
- Korean Spicy Beef Ramen
- Sesame Ginger Ramen with Tofu
- Spicy Crab Ramen
- Turkey Ramen with Cranberry Sauce
- Creamy Coconut Curry Ramen
- Buffalo Chicken Ramen

Classic Shoyu Ramen

Ingredients:

For the broth:

- 8 cups water
- 4 cups vegetable broth
- 1 onion, peeled and halved
- 4 cloves garlic, smashed
- 2-inch piece of ginger, sliced
- 1 cup sliced mushrooms (shiitake or cremini)
- 2 tablespoons soy sauce
- 2 tablespoons mirin
- 1 tablespoon sesame oil
- Salt, to taste

For the noodles and toppings:

- 4 packs of ramen noodles
- 4 soft-boiled eggs, peeled and halved
- 2 cups baby spinach or bok choy
- 2 green onions, thinly sliced
- Nori seaweed sheets, torn into small pieces
- Sesame seeds, for garnish
- Chili oil or hot sauce (optional)

Instructions:

In a large pot, combine the water, vegetable broth, onion, garlic, ginger, mushrooms, soy sauce, mirin, and sesame oil. Bring to a boil over high heat. Once boiling, reduce the heat to low and let the broth simmer for about 30-40 minutes to allow the flavors to meld together. Taste and adjust seasoning with salt if needed.

While the broth is simmering, prepare the toppings. Cook the ramen noodles according to the package instructions. Drain and set aside.

In a separate pot, blanch the spinach or bok choy in boiling water for about 1-2 minutes until wilted. Drain and set aside.

Soft-boil the eggs by placing them in a pot of boiling water for about 6-7 minutes. Transfer to a bowl of ice water to stop the cooking process, then peel and halve them.

Once the broth is ready, strain it through a fine mesh sieve, discarding the solids. Taste the broth again and adjust seasoning if needed.

To assemble the ramen bowls, divide the cooked noodles among serving bowls. Ladle the hot broth over the noodles.

Arrange the soft-boiled egg halves, blanched spinach or bok choy, sliced green onions, torn nori seaweed, and sesame seeds on top of each bowl.

Optionally, drizzle some chili oil or hot sauce over the ramen for extra heat.

Serve the Classic Shoyu Ramen hot and enjoy!

This recipe yields a delicious and comforting bowl of ramen with a savory soy-based broth, perfect for any day of the week. Feel free to customize the toppings to your preference!

Miso Ramen with Tofu and Mushrooms

Ingredients:

For the broth:

- 8 cups vegetable broth
- 4 cloves garlic, minced
- 2-inch piece of ginger, sliced
- 1/4 cup white miso paste
- 2 tablespoons soy sauce
- 2 tablespoons mirin
- 1 tablespoon sesame oil
- Salt and pepper, to taste

For the tofu and mushrooms:

- 1 block firm tofu, pressed and cubed
- 2 cups sliced mushrooms (shiitake, cremini, or your choice)
- 2 tablespoons soy sauce
- 1 tablespoon sesame oil

For the ramen:

- 4 packs of ramen noodles
- 2 cups baby spinach or bok choy
- 4 soft-boiled eggs, peeled and halved
- 2 green onions, thinly sliced
- Nori seaweed sheets, torn into small pieces
- Sesame seeds, for garnish
- Chili oil or hot sauce (optional)

Instructions:

In a large pot, combine the vegetable broth, minced garlic, sliced ginger, white miso paste, soy sauce, mirin, and sesame oil. Bring to a simmer over medium heat.

Let the broth simmer for about 15-20 minutes to allow the flavors to meld together. Taste and adjust seasoning with salt and pepper if needed.

While the broth is simmering, prepare the tofu and mushrooms. In a skillet, heat the sesame oil over medium heat. Add the cubed tofu and sliced mushrooms, and sauté until the tofu is golden brown and the mushrooms are tender, about 8-10 minutes. Stir in the soy sauce and cook for another 2-3 minutes. Set aside.

Cook the ramen noodles according to the package instructions. Drain and set aside.

Blanch the baby spinach or bok choy in boiling water for about 1-2 minutes until wilted. Drain and set aside.

To assemble the ramen bowls, divide the cooked noodles among serving bowls. Ladle the hot miso broth over the noodles.

Arrange the sautéed tofu and mushrooms, soft-boiled egg halves, blanched spinach or bok choy, sliced green onions, torn nori seaweed, and sesame seeds on top of each bowl.

Optionally, drizzle some chili oil or hot sauce over the ramen for extra heat.

Serve the Miso Ramen with Tofu and Mushrooms hot and enjoy!

This flavorful and satisfying ramen is perfect for cozy nights in. Feel free to adjust the toppings and seasonings to suit your taste preferences.

Spicy Kimchi Ramen

Ingredients:

For the broth:

- 6 cups vegetable broth
- 1 cup kimchi, chopped
- 2 tablespoons kimchi juice (from the jar)
- 3 cloves garlic, minced
- 2 tablespoons soy sauce
- 1 tablespoon gochujang (Korean chili paste)
- 1 tablespoon sesame oil
- 1 tablespoon rice vinegar
- Salt and pepper, to taste

For the ramen:

- 4 packs of ramen noodles
- 1 cup sliced mushrooms (shiitake, cremini, or your choice)
- 1 cup sliced green onions
- 1 cup shredded cabbage
- 4 soft-boiled eggs, peeled and halved
- Toasted sesame seeds, for garnish
- Nori seaweed sheets, torn into small pieces, for garnish

Instructions:

In a large pot, combine the vegetable broth, chopped kimchi, kimchi juice, minced garlic, soy sauce, gochujang, sesame oil, and rice vinegar. Bring to a simmer over medium heat.

Let the broth simmer for about 15-20 minutes to allow the flavors to meld together. Taste and adjust seasoning with salt and pepper if needed.

While the broth is simmering, prepare the ramen toppings. Cook the ramen noodles according to the package instructions. Drain and set aside.

In the same pot used for the broth, add the sliced mushrooms and shredded cabbage. Cook for 2-3 minutes until they start to soften.

To assemble the ramen bowls, divide the cooked noodles among serving bowls. Ladle the hot kimchi broth over the noodles.

Top each bowl with the cooked mushrooms, shredded cabbage, sliced green onions, and soft-boiled egg halves.
Garnish each bowl with toasted sesame seeds and torn nori seaweed.
Serve the Spicy Kimchi Ramen hot and enjoy!

This spicy and flavorful ramen is perfect for kimchi lovers and those who enjoy a bit of heat in their meals. Adjust the level of spiciness by adding more or less gochujang according to your preference.

Vegetarian Ramen with Roasted Vegetables

Ingredients:

For the broth:

- 6 cups vegetable broth
- 3 cloves garlic, minced
- 2-inch piece of ginger, sliced
- 2 tablespoons soy sauce
- 1 tablespoon sesame oil
- 1 tablespoon rice vinegar
- Salt and pepper, to taste

For the roasted vegetables:

- 2 cups mixed vegetables, such as bell peppers, broccoli, carrots, and mushrooms, cut into bite-sized pieces
- 2 tablespoons olive oil
- 1 tablespoon soy sauce
- 1 tablespoon maple syrup or honey (optional)
- Salt and pepper, to taste

For the ramen:

- 4 packs of ramen noodles
- 2 cups baby spinach or bok choy
- 1 cup sliced green onions
- 1 cup bean sprouts (optional)
- 4 soft-boiled eggs, peeled and halved (optional)
- Toasted sesame seeds, for garnish
- Nori seaweed sheets, torn into small pieces, for garnish

Instructions:

Preheat your oven to 400°F (200°C). Line a baking sheet with parchment paper. In a large bowl, toss the mixed vegetables with olive oil, soy sauce, maple syrup or honey (if using), salt, and pepper until well coated.

Spread the vegetables in a single layer on the prepared baking sheet. Roast in the preheated oven for 20-25 minutes, or until the vegetables are tender and slightly caramelized.

In a large pot, combine the vegetable broth, minced garlic, sliced ginger, soy sauce, sesame oil, rice vinegar, salt, and pepper. Bring to a simmer over medium heat.

Let the broth simmer for about 15-20 minutes to allow the flavors to meld together. Taste and adjust seasoning with salt and pepper if needed.

While the broth is simmering, cook the ramen noodles according to the package instructions. Drain and set aside.

To assemble the ramen bowls, divide the cooked noodles among serving bowls. Ladle the hot broth over the noodles.

Top each bowl with the roasted vegetables, baby spinach or bok choy, sliced green onions, and bean sprouts (if using).

Optionally, add soft-boiled egg halves to each bowl.

Garnish each bowl with toasted sesame seeds and torn nori seaweed.

Serve the Vegetarian Ramen with Roasted Vegetables hot and enjoy!

This hearty and nutritious ramen is packed with flavor and makes for a satisfying meal. Customize the roasted vegetables according to your preference and seasonal availability.

Tonkotsu Ramen with Pork Belly

Ingredients:

For the broth:

- 8 cups water
- 4 cups chicken broth
- 1 pound pork bones (such as pork neck bones or pork trotters)
- 2 cloves garlic, crushed
- 2-inch piece of ginger, sliced
- 2 green onions, chopped
- 1 tablespoon soy sauce
- 1 tablespoon sesame oil
- Salt, to taste

For the pork belly:

- 1 pound pork belly
- 2 tablespoons soy sauce
- 2 tablespoons mirin
- 1 tablespoon sesame oil
- 1 tablespoon sugar
- 2 cloves garlic, minced
- 1-inch piece of ginger, grated

For the ramen:

- 4 packs of ramen noodles
- 4 soft-boiled eggs, peeled and halved
- 2 cups baby spinach or bok choy
- 2 cups sliced mushrooms (shiitake, cremini, or your choice)
- 2 green onions, thinly sliced
- Nori seaweed sheets, torn into small pieces
- Toasted sesame seeds, for garnish

Instructions:

In a large pot, combine the water, chicken broth, pork bones, crushed garlic, sliced ginger, chopped green onions, soy sauce, sesame oil, and salt. Bring to a boil over high heat.

Once boiling, reduce the heat to low and let the broth simmer for about 6-8 hours, stirring occasionally. Skim off any foam and impurities that rise to the surface.

While the broth is simmering, prepare the pork belly. In a bowl, mix together the soy sauce, mirin, sesame oil, sugar, minced garlic, and grated ginger. Add the pork belly to the marinade, making sure it's well coated. Cover and refrigerate for at least 1 hour, or overnight.

After marinating, preheat your oven to 350°F (175°C). Place the pork belly on a baking sheet lined with foil. Roast in the preheated oven for 45-50 minutes, or until the pork belly is tender and caramelized. Remove from the oven and let it rest for a few minutes before slicing thinly.

Cook the ramen noodles according to the package instructions. Drain and set aside.

To assemble the ramen bowls, divide the cooked noodles among serving bowls. Ladle the hot tonkotsu broth over the noodles.

Arrange the sliced pork belly, soft-boiled egg halves, baby spinach or bok choy, sliced mushrooms, and thinly sliced green onions on top of each bowl.

Garnish each bowl with torn nori seaweed and toasted sesame seeds.

Serve the Tonkotsu Ramen with Pork Belly hot and enjoy!

This rich and flavorful ramen is a classic Japanese favorite. The creamy tonkotsu broth pairs perfectly with the tender pork belly and other toppings. Adjust the seasoning and toppings according to your preference.

Vegan Ramen with Seared Tofu

Ingredients:

- 4 packs of ramen noodles (ensure they are vegan-friendly)
- 1 block of firm tofu, pressed and drained
- 4 cups vegetable broth
- 1 tablespoon soy sauce
- 1 tablespoon miso paste
- 1 tablespoon sesame oil
- 2 cloves garlic, minced
- 1-inch piece of ginger, grated
- 2 cups sliced mushrooms (shiitake or cremini work well)
- 2 cups baby spinach
- 2 green onions, sliced
- 1 sheet of nori, sliced into thin strips (optional)
- Sriracha or chili oil for garnish (optional)

Instructions:

Start by preparing the tofu. Slice the tofu into cubes or rectangles, whichever shape you prefer. Heat a non-stick skillet over medium-high heat and add a bit of oil. Once the skillet is hot, add the tofu pieces and sear on each side until golden brown and crispy. This should take about 3-4 minutes per side. Once done, set the tofu aside.

In a large pot, heat the sesame oil over medium heat. Add the minced garlic and grated ginger, and sauté for about 1 minute until fragrant.

Pour in the vegetable broth and bring it to a simmer. Stir in the soy sauce and miso paste until well combined. Let it simmer for about 5 minutes to allow the flavors to meld.

Meanwhile, cook the ramen noodles according to the package instructions. Drain and set aside.

Add the sliced mushrooms to the broth and let them cook for 2-3 minutes until softened.

Once the mushrooms are cooked, add the baby spinach to the pot and let it wilt for about 1-2 minutes.

To assemble the ramen bowls, divide the cooked noodles among serving bowls. Ladle the hot broth and vegetables over the noodles.

Top each bowl with the seared tofu, sliced green onions, and nori strips if using.
You can also add a drizzle of sriracha or chili oil for some extra heat.
Serve immediately and enjoy your delicious vegan ramen with seared tofu!

Feel free to adjust the seasoning and add other vegetables or toppings according to your preference. Enjoy your meal!

Chicken Ramen with Soft-Boiled Egg

Ingredients:

- 4 packs of ramen noodles
- 4 cups chicken broth
- 2 boneless, skinless chicken breasts
- 4 large eggs
- 1 tablespoon soy sauce
- 1 tablespoon mirin (Japanese sweet rice wine)
- 1 tablespoon sesame oil
- 2 cloves garlic, minced
- 1-inch piece of ginger, grated
- 2 cups sliced mushrooms (shiitake or cremini work well)
- 2 cups baby spinach
- 2 green onions, sliced
- 1 sheet of nori, sliced into thin strips (optional)
- Salt and pepper to taste

Instructions:

In a pot, bring water to a boil. Once boiling, carefully add the eggs and cook for 6-7 minutes for a soft-boiled egg. Once done, remove the eggs with a slotted spoon and transfer them to a bowl of ice water to stop the cooking process. Peel the eggs and set them aside.

In another pot, bring the chicken broth to a simmer over medium heat.

In a separate skillet, heat the sesame oil over medium heat. Add the minced garlic and grated ginger, and sauté for about 1 minute until fragrant.

Add the sliced mushrooms to the skillet and cook until they are softened, about 3-4 minutes.

Season the chicken breasts with salt and pepper, then add them to the skillet with the mushrooms. Cook for about 5-6 minutes on each side, or until fully cooked through. Remove the chicken from the skillet and let it rest for a few minutes before slicing it thinly.

While the chicken is cooking, cook the ramen noodles according to the package instructions. Drain and set aside.

Stir the soy sauce and mirin into the simmering chicken broth.

To assemble the ramen bowls, divide the cooked noodles among serving bowls. Ladle the hot broth over the noodles.

Top each bowl with slices of the cooked chicken, a soft-boiled egg cut in half, sliced green onions, and nori strips if using.
Serve immediately and enjoy your delicious chicken ramen with soft-boiled egg!

Feel free to adjust the seasoning and add other vegetables or toppings according to your preference. Enjoy your meal!

Thai Coconut Curry Ramen

Ingredients:

- 4 packs of ramen noodles
- 1 can (14 oz) coconut milk
- 4 cups vegetable broth
- 2 tablespoons Thai red curry paste
- 2 tablespoons soy sauce
- 1 tablespoon coconut sugar or brown sugar
- 2 cloves garlic, minced
- 1 tablespoon grated ginger
- 1 red bell pepper, thinly sliced
- 1 carrot, julienned
- 1 cup sliced mushrooms (shiitake or cremini)
- 1 cup baby spinach
- 1 block tofu, cubed and pressed to remove excess water
- Juice of 1 lime
- Salt and pepper to taste
- Optional toppings: chopped cilantro, sliced green onions, lime wedges, chili flakes

Instructions:

In a large pot, combine the coconut milk, vegetable broth, Thai red curry paste, soy sauce, and coconut sugar. Bring the mixture to a simmer over medium heat, stirring to combine all the ingredients.

Add the minced garlic and grated ginger to the pot, and let it simmer for a few minutes to allow the flavors to meld.

Add the sliced red bell pepper, julienned carrot, and sliced mushrooms to the pot. Let them cook for about 5-7 minutes, until they begin to soften.

While the vegetables are cooking, prepare the tofu. Heat a non-stick skillet over medium-high heat and add a bit of oil. Once the skillet is hot, add the tofu cubes and cook until they are golden brown and crispy on all sides, about 5-7 minutes. Set aside.

Cook the ramen noodles according to the package instructions. Drain and set aside.

Once the vegetables are tender, add the baby spinach to the pot and let it wilt for about 1-2 minutes.

Stir in the lime juice, and season the broth with salt and pepper to taste.

To assemble the ramen bowls, divide the cooked noodles among serving bowls.

Ladle the hot coconut curry broth and vegetables over the noodles.

Top each bowl with the crispy tofu cubes and any optional toppings you like, such as chopped cilantro, sliced green onions, lime wedges, or chili flakes.

Serve immediately and enjoy your flavorful Thai Coconut Curry Ramen!

Feel free to adjust the spiciness of the curry paste according to your preference, and

add more vegetables or protein if desired. Enjoy your meal!

Spicy Pork Ramen with Bok Choy

Ingredients:

For the broth:

- 4 packs of ramen noodles
- 6 cups chicken or pork broth
- 2 tablespoons soy sauce
- 2 tablespoons sesame oil
- 2 tablespoons mirin (Japanese sweet rice wine)
- 2 tablespoons chili paste or sriracha sauce (adjust to taste)
- 2 cloves garlic, minced
- 1 tablespoon grated ginger
- Salt and pepper to taste

For the pork:

- 1 lb pork shoulder or pork belly, thinly sliced
- 2 tablespoons soy sauce
- 1 tablespoon sesame oil
- 1 tablespoon honey or brown sugar
- 2 cloves garlic, minced
- 1 tablespoon grated ginger
- 2 tablespoons vegetable oil

For the toppings:

- 4 heads baby bok choy, halved
- 4 soft-boiled eggs
- 2 green onions, thinly sliced
- Sesame seeds for garnish

Instructions:

In a large pot, combine the chicken or pork broth, soy sauce, sesame oil, mirin, chili paste or sriracha, minced garlic, and grated ginger. Bring the mixture to a simmer over medium heat, then reduce the heat to low and let it simmer for about 20-30 minutes to allow the flavors to meld. Season with salt and pepper to taste.

While the broth is simmering, prepare the pork. In a bowl, combine the sliced pork with soy sauce, sesame oil, honey or brown sugar, minced garlic, and grated ginger. Toss to coat the pork evenly.

Heat vegetable oil in a skillet over medium-high heat. Add the marinated pork slices and cook for about 2-3 minutes on each side until they are golden brown and cooked through. Remove the pork from the skillet and set aside.

In the same skillet, add the halved baby bok choy and cook for about 2-3 minutes on each side until they are tender and slightly charred. Remove from the skillet and set aside.

Cook the ramen noodles according to the package instructions. Drain and set aside.

To assemble the ramen bowls, divide the cooked noodles among serving bowls. Ladle the hot broth over the noodles.

Top each bowl with slices of the cooked pork, halved baby bok choy, soft-boiled egg, sliced green onions, and sesame seeds.

Serve immediately and enjoy your spicy pork ramen with bok choy!

Feel free to adjust the spiciness of the broth according to your preference, and add other toppings like sliced mushrooms or corn kernels if desired. Enjoy your meal!

Garlic Shrimp Ramen

Ingredients:

For the garlic shrimp:

- 1 lb large shrimp, peeled and deveined
- 4 cloves garlic, minced
- 2 tablespoons olive oil
- Salt and pepper to taste
- Crushed red pepper flakes (optional)

For the broth:

- 4 packs of ramen noodles
- 6 cups seafood or chicken broth
- 2 tablespoons soy sauce
- 1 tablespoon sesame oil
- 1 tablespoon rice vinegar
- 1 tablespoon mirin (optional)
- 1 tablespoon grated ginger
- 2 cloves garlic, minced

For the toppings:

- 2 cups baby spinach
- 2 green onions, thinly sliced
- Sesame seeds for garnish
- Sliced nori (optional)

Instructions:

In a large pot, bring the seafood or chicken broth to a simmer over medium heat. Add soy sauce, sesame oil, rice vinegar, mirin (if using), minced garlic, and grated ginger. Let the broth simmer for about 10-15 minutes to allow the flavors to meld. Season with salt and pepper to taste.

While the broth is simmering, heat olive oil in a skillet over medium heat. Add minced garlic and cook until fragrant, about 1 minute.

Add the shrimp to the skillet and cook for 2-3 minutes on each side until they turn pink and opaque. Season with salt, pepper, and crushed red pepper flakes if you like some heat. Once cooked, set the shrimp aside.

Cook the ramen noodles according to the package instructions. Drain and set aside.

To assemble the ramen bowls, divide the cooked noodles among serving bowls. Ladle the hot broth over the noodles.

Add a handful of baby spinach to each bowl. The hot broth will wilt the spinach.

Top each bowl with the cooked garlic shrimp, sliced green onions, sesame seeds, and sliced nori if using.

Serve immediately and enjoy your delicious garlic shrimp ramen!

Feel free to customize your ramen with additional toppings such as soft-boiled eggs, sliced mushrooms, or bamboo shoots. Enjoy your meal!

Beef Ramen with Stir-Fried Vegetables

Ingredients:

For the beef marinade:

- 1 lb flank steak, thinly sliced
- 2 tablespoons soy sauce
- 1 tablespoon sesame oil
- 1 tablespoon mirin (Japanese sweet rice wine) or rice vinegar
- 2 cloves garlic, minced
- 1 tablespoon grated ginger
- 1 teaspoon cornstarch

For the stir-fried vegetables:

- 2 tablespoons vegetable oil
- 2 cups mixed vegetables (such as bell peppers, carrots, broccoli florets, snap peas)
- 2 cloves garlic, minced
- 1 tablespoon soy sauce
- 1 tablespoon oyster sauce (optional)
- Salt and pepper to taste

For the ramen:

- 4 packs of ramen noodles
- 6 cups beef broth
- 2 tablespoons soy sauce
- 2 teaspoons sesame oil
- 2 teaspoons mirin (optional)
- Salt and pepper to taste

Optional toppings:

- Sliced green onions
- Sesame seeds
- Chili flakes
- Soft-boiled eggs

Instructions:

In a bowl, combine the thinly sliced flank steak with soy sauce, sesame oil, mirin, minced garlic, grated ginger, and cornstarch. Toss to coat the beef evenly. Let it marinate for at least 15-20 minutes.

Heat 1 tablespoon of vegetable oil in a large skillet or wok over high heat. Add the marinated beef slices in a single layer and cook for about 1-2 minutes per side until browned and slightly caramelized. Remove the beef from the skillet and set aside.

In the same skillet, heat another tablespoon of vegetable oil over medium-high heat. Add the mixed vegetables and minced garlic. Stir-fry for about 3-4 minutes until the vegetables are crisp-tender.

Add soy sauce and oyster sauce to the skillet, if using. Stir well to coat the vegetables evenly. Season with salt and pepper to taste. Remove the vegetables from the skillet and set aside.

In a large pot, bring the beef broth to a simmer over medium heat. Stir in soy sauce, sesame oil, and mirin. Season with salt and pepper to taste.

Cook the ramen noodles according to the package instructions. Drain and set aside.

To assemble the ramen bowls, divide the cooked noodles among serving bowls. Ladle the hot beef broth over the noodles.

Top each bowl with slices of the cooked beef and stir-fried vegetables.

Garnish with sliced green onions, sesame seeds, and chili flakes if desired. You can also add a soft-boiled egg to each bowl if you like.

Serve immediately and enjoy your delicious beef ramen with stir-fried vegetables!

Feel free to customize the vegetables according to your preference, and adjust the seasoning of the broth to suit your taste. Enjoy your meal!

Sesame Soy Ramen with Spinach

Ingredients:

- 2 packs of ramen noodles (about 200g)
- 4 cups water
- 2 tablespoons soy sauce
- 1 tablespoon sesame oil
- 2 cloves garlic, minced
- 1 teaspoon grated ginger
- 2 cups fresh spinach leaves
- Optional toppings: sliced green onions, sesame seeds, soft-boiled egg, sliced mushrooms

Instructions:

Cook the ramen noodles according to package instructions. Drain and set aside.
In a pot, bring water to a boil. Add minced garlic and grated ginger.
Stir in soy sauce and sesame oil.
Add the fresh spinach leaves to the pot and let them wilt for about 1-2 minutes.
Once the spinach has wilted, add the cooked ramen noodles to the pot.
Stir everything together until the noodles are heated through and well coated with the sauce.
Serve hot, garnished with sliced green onions, sesame seeds, and any other desired toppings.

Enjoy your delicious Sesame Soy Ramen with Spinach!

Hawaiian Poke Ramen Bowl

Ingredients:

- 2 packs of ramen noodles (about 200g)
- 4 cups water
- 1/4 cup soy sauce
- 2 tablespoons rice vinegar
- 1 tablespoon sesame oil
- 1 tablespoon honey
- 1 teaspoon grated ginger
- 2 cloves garlic, minced
- 1 cup diced sushi-grade tuna or salmon
- 1/2 cup diced cucumber
- 1/2 cup diced avocado
- 1/4 cup sliced green onions
- 1/4 cup chopped seaweed (optional)
- 1/4 cup diced pineapple
- Sesame seeds for garnish
- Sliced jalapeno for garnish (optional)

Instructions:

Cook the ramen noodles according to package instructions. Drain and set aside.
In a pot, bring water to a boil. Add minced garlic and grated ginger.
Stir in soy sauce, rice vinegar, sesame oil, and honey. Let simmer for 2-3 minutes.
In a bowl, combine the diced tuna or salmon, cucumber, avocado, green onions,
chopped seaweed (if using), and diced pineapple.
Divide the cooked ramen noodles into serving bowls.
Pour the hot broth over the noodles in each bowl.
Top each bowl with the poke mixture.
Garnish with sesame seeds and sliced jalapeno if desired.
Serve immediately and enjoy your Hawaiian Poke Ramen Bowl!

Feel free to adjust the ingredients and proportions according to your taste preferences.

Szechuan Spicy Ramen

Ingredients:

- 2 packs of ramen noodles (about 200g)
- 4 cups water
- 2 tablespoons sesame oil
- 2 tablespoons soy sauce
- 2 tablespoons Szechuan chili bean paste (doubanjiang)
- 2 teaspoons chili oil (adjust to taste for spice level)
- 2 teaspoons grated ginger
- 2 cloves garlic, minced
- 2 cups sliced bok choy or napa cabbage
- 1/2 cup sliced mushrooms (shiitake or button mushrooms work well)
- 1/2 cup sliced bell peppers (red or green)
- 1/4 cup sliced green onions
- Optional toppings: soft-boiled egg, sliced tofu, shredded chicken, sesame seeds, chopped cilantro

Instructions:

Cook the ramen noodles according to package instructions. Drain and set aside.
In a pot, heat sesame oil over medium heat. Add minced garlic and grated ginger, and sauté for about 1 minute until fragrant.
Stir in the Szechuan chili bean paste (doubanjiang) and chili oil. Cook for another minute.
Pour in the water and soy sauce. Bring the mixture to a simmer.
Add the sliced mushrooms and bell peppers to the pot. Let simmer for about 3-4 minutes until the vegetables are slightly tender.
Add the sliced bok choy or napa cabbage to the pot and cook for another 1-2 minutes until wilted.
Divide the cooked ramen noodles into serving bowls.
Ladle the spicy broth and vegetables over the noodles in each bowl.
Top each bowl with sliced green onions and any optional toppings you desire.
Serve hot and enjoy your Szechuan Spicy Ramen!

Adjust the amount of chili oil and chili bean paste according to your preferred level of spiciness. You can also customize the toppings to your liking.

Smoked Salmon Ramen

Ingredients:

- 2 packs of ramen noodles (about 200g)
- 4 cups chicken or vegetable broth
- 1 tablespoon soy sauce
- 1 tablespoon miso paste
- 1 teaspoon grated ginger
- 2 cloves garlic, minced
- 1 cup sliced shiitake mushrooms
- 2 cups baby spinach leaves
- 1 cup smoked salmon, flaked
- 2 soft-boiled eggs, halved
- 1 sheet nori (seaweed), cut into thin strips
- Sliced green onions for garnish
- Sesame seeds for garnish
- Optional: Sriracha or chili oil for extra heat

Instructions:

Cook the ramen noodles according to package instructions. Drain and set aside.
In a pot, heat the chicken or vegetable broth over medium heat.
Stir in soy sauce, miso paste, grated ginger, and minced garlic. Allow the broth to simmer for about 5 minutes to let the flavors meld.
Add the sliced shiitake mushrooms to the broth and cook for 2-3 minutes until they soften.
Add the baby spinach leaves to the pot and cook for an additional 1-2 minutes until they wilt.
Divide the cooked ramen noodles into serving bowls.
Ladle the hot broth and vegetables over the noodles in each bowl.
Top each bowl with flaked smoked salmon, soft-boiled egg halves, and nori strips.
Garnish with sliced green onions and sesame seeds.
Optionally, drizzle some Sriracha or chili oil over the ramen for extra heat.
Serve hot and enjoy your Smoked Salmon Ramen!

Feel free to adjust the ingredients and toppings according to your preferences. This recipe provides a delicious fusion of flavors with the smoky richness of the salmon complementing the savory broth and noodles.

Teriyaki Chicken Ramen

Ingredients:

- 2 boneless, skinless chicken breasts
- Salt and pepper, to taste
- 2 packs of ramen noodles (about 200g)
- 4 cups chicken broth
- 3 tablespoons soy sauce
- 2 tablespoons mirin (Japanese sweet rice wine)
- 2 tablespoons brown sugar
- 1 tablespoon sesame oil
- 2 cloves garlic, minced
- 1 teaspoon grated ginger
- 2 cups chopped bok choy or spinach
- 1 carrot, julienned
- 1/4 cup sliced green onions
- Sesame seeds for garnish
- Optional: Sriracha or chili flakes for extra heat

Instructions:

Season the chicken breasts with salt and pepper on both sides.
Heat a skillet or grill pan over medium-high heat. Cook the chicken breasts for about 6-8 minutes on each side until fully cooked and juices run clear. Remove from heat and let rest for a few minutes before slicing thinly.
In a pot, bring the chicken broth to a boil. Add soy sauce, mirin, brown sugar, sesame oil, minced garlic, and grated ginger. Stir well to combine and let simmer for 5 minutes.
Cook the ramen noodles according to package instructions. Drain and set aside.
Add the chopped bok choy or spinach and julienned carrot to the pot with the broth. Cook for about 2-3 minutes until the vegetables are tender-crisp.
Divide the cooked ramen noodles into serving bowls.
Ladle the hot broth and vegetables over the noodles in each bowl.
Top each bowl with sliced teriyaki chicken.
Garnish with sliced green onions and sesame seeds.
Optionally, add a drizzle of Sriracha or sprinkle of chili flakes for extra heat.
Serve hot and enjoy your Teriyaki Chicken Ramen!

This recipe offers a comforting and flavorful bowl of ramen with tender teriyaki chicken and savory broth. Feel free to customize it with your favorite vegetables or additional toppings.

Creamy Pumpkin Ramen

Ingredients:

- 2 packs of ramen noodles (about 200g)
- 4 cups vegetable broth
- 1 cup canned pumpkin puree
- 1 cup coconut milk
- 2 cloves garlic, minced
- 1 tablespoon grated ginger
- 2 tablespoons soy sauce
- 1 tablespoon maple syrup or honey
- 1 tablespoon sesame oil
- 1 teaspoon ground cinnamon
- 1/2 teaspoon ground nutmeg
- Salt and pepper to taste
- Sliced green onions for garnish
- Optional toppings: roasted pumpkin seeds, sliced mushrooms, shredded chicken, crispy tofu

Instructions:

In a pot, combine vegetable broth, canned pumpkin puree, coconut milk, minced garlic, grated ginger, soy sauce, maple syrup or honey, sesame oil, ground cinnamon, and ground nutmeg. Stir well to combine.

Place the pot over medium heat and bring the mixture to a simmer. Let it simmer for about 10 minutes, stirring occasionally.

While the broth simmers, cook the ramen noodles according to package instructions. Drain and set aside.

Once the broth is ready, taste and adjust seasoning with salt and pepper as needed.

Divide the cooked ramen noodles into serving bowls.

Ladle the hot creamy pumpkin broth over the noodles in each bowl.

Garnish with sliced green onions and any other desired toppings, such as roasted pumpkin seeds, sliced mushrooms, shredded chicken, or crispy tofu.

Serve hot and enjoy your Creamy Pumpkin Ramen!

This recipe offers a comforting and creamy twist to traditional ramen, with the sweetness of pumpkin complemented by warm spices like cinnamon and nutmeg. Feel free to customize it with your favorite toppings and adjust the seasoning to your taste preferences.

Ramen Carbonara

Ingredients:

- 2 packs of ramen noodles (about 200g)
- 4 slices of bacon, chopped
- 2 cloves garlic, minced
- 2 large eggs
- 1/2 cup grated Parmesan cheese
- Salt and black pepper to taste
- Chopped parsley for garnish

Instructions:

Cook the ramen noodles according to package instructions. Drain and set aside.
In a large skillet, cook the chopped bacon over medium heat until crispy. Remove the bacon from the skillet and set it aside, leaving the bacon fat in the skillet.
In the same skillet with the bacon fat, add minced garlic and cook for about 1 minute until fragrant.
In a mixing bowl, whisk together the eggs and grated Parmesan cheese until well combined.
Add the cooked ramen noodles to the skillet with the garlic and bacon fat. Toss to coat the noodles evenly with the garlic-infused fat.
Remove the skillet from the heat. Quickly pour the egg and Parmesan mixture over the hot noodles while continuously tossing the noodles to coat them with the creamy sauce. The residual heat from the noodles will cook the eggs, creating a creamy sauce.
Once the noodles are coated with the sauce and the sauce thickens slightly, season with salt and black pepper to taste.
Add the crispy bacon back to the skillet and toss to combine.
Divide the Ramen Carbonara into serving bowls. Garnish with chopped parsley.
Serve immediately and enjoy your Ramen Carbonara!

This recipe offers a unique twist on the classic carbonara pasta dish, with the addition of ramen noodles for a comforting and satisfying meal. Feel free to customize it by adding other ingredients like sautéed mushrooms or peas if desired.

Lobster Ramen with Miso Broth

Ingredients:

- 2 lobster tails (about 8-10 oz each)
- 2 packs of ramen noodles (about 200g)
- 4 cups seafood or vegetable broth
- 2 tablespoons white miso paste
- 1 tablespoon soy sauce
- 1 tablespoon mirin (Japanese sweet rice wine)
- 1 tablespoon sesame oil
- 2 cloves garlic, minced
- 1 teaspoon grated ginger
- 2 cups baby spinach leaves
- 1 cup sliced shiitake mushrooms
- 1/4 cup sliced green onions
- Sesame seeds for garnish
- Optional: Sriracha or chili oil for extra heat

Instructions:

Preheat your oven to 400°F (200°C).

Prepare the lobster tails by cutting them open along the top shell and gently pulling the meat upward, leaving it attached at the tail end. Place the lobster tails on a baking sheet.

In a small bowl, mix together minced garlic, grated ginger, soy sauce, mirin, and sesame oil. Brush this mixture generously over the lobster meat.

Bake the lobster tails in the preheated oven for about 10-12 minutes until the meat is opaque and cooked through.

While the lobster is baking, in a pot, bring the seafood or vegetable broth to a simmer over medium heat.

In a small bowl, whisk together the white miso paste with a ladleful of hot broth until smooth. Pour this miso mixture back into the pot of simmering broth.

Cook the ramen noodles according to package instructions. Drain and set aside.

Add the baby spinach leaves and sliced shiitake mushrooms to the pot of miso broth. Let simmer for about 2-3 minutes until the vegetables are tender.

Divide the cooked ramen noodles into serving bowls.

Ladle the hot miso broth and vegetables over the noodles in each bowl.

Once the lobster tails are done baking, remove them from the oven and slice the meat into medallions. Place the lobster meat on top of each bowl of ramen.
Garnish each bowl with sliced green onions and sesame seeds.
Optionally, drizzle some Sriracha or chili oil over the ramen for extra heat.
Serve hot and enjoy your Lobster Ramen with Miso Broth!

This recipe offers a sophisticated and flavorful twist on traditional ramen, with

succulent lobster meat and umami-rich miso broth. Adjust the seasoning and spice

level according to your taste preferences.

Lemon Ginger Chicken Ramen

Ingredients:

- 2 packs of ramen noodles (about 200g)
- 4 cups chicken broth
- 2 boneless, skinless chicken breasts
- Salt and pepper to taste
- 2 tablespoons soy sauce
- 2 tablespoons freshly squeezed lemon juice
- 1 tablespoon honey
- 1 tablespoon grated ginger
- 2 cloves garlic, minced
- Zest of 1 lemon
- 2 cups baby spinach leaves
- 1 cup sliced shiitake mushrooms
- 2 green onions, thinly sliced
- Sesame seeds for garnish
- Sliced chili pepper for garnish (optional)

Instructions:

Season the chicken breasts with salt and pepper on both sides.
In a large skillet or pot, heat some oil over medium-high heat. Add the chicken breasts and cook for about 6-8 minutes on each side until fully cooked and no longer pink in the center. Remove the chicken from the skillet and let it rest for a few minutes before slicing thinly.
In the same skillet or pot, add minced garlic and grated ginger. Cook for about 1 minute until fragrant.
Pour in the chicken broth, soy sauce, lemon juice, and honey. Stir well to combine.
Bring the broth to a simmer. Add the sliced shiitake mushrooms and baby spinach leaves. Let simmer for about 2-3 minutes until the vegetables are tender.
Meanwhile, cook the ramen noodles according to package instructions. Drain and set aside.
Once the vegetables are tender, add the cooked ramen noodles to the pot.
Stir in the lemon zest and sliced green onions. Taste and adjust seasoning if needed.
Divide the Lemon Ginger Chicken Ramen into serving bowls.

Top each bowl with thinly sliced chicken breast.
Garnish with sesame seeds and sliced chili pepper if desired.
Serve hot and enjoy your Lemon Ginger Chicken Ramen!

This recipe offers a delightful blend of tangy lemon, aromatic ginger, and savory chicken, creating a comforting and refreshing bowl of ramen. Feel free to customize it with your favorite vegetables or additional garnishes.

Spicy Tofu Ramen with Sriracha

Ingredients:

- 2 packs of ramen noodles (about 200g)
- 4 cups vegetable broth
- 1 block (about 14 oz) firm tofu, pressed and cubed
- 2 tablespoons soy sauce
- 1 tablespoon sesame oil
- 1 tablespoon grated ginger
- 2 cloves garlic, minced
- 2 tablespoons Sriracha sauce (adjust to taste)
- 2 cups sliced shiitake mushrooms
- 2 cups baby spinach leaves
- 2 green onions, thinly sliced
- Sesame seeds for garnish
- Optional: Soft-boiled eggs, sliced chili pepper for extra heat

Instructions:

Press the tofu to remove excess moisture. Cut the tofu into cubes.
In a large skillet or wok, heat some oil over medium-high heat. Add the cubed tofu and cook until golden brown on all sides. Remove the tofu from the skillet and set it aside.
In the same skillet or wok, add minced garlic and grated ginger. Cook for about 1 minute until fragrant.
Pour in the vegetable broth and bring it to a simmer.
Stir in soy sauce, sesame oil, and Sriracha sauce. Adjust the amount of Sriracha according to your desired level of spiciness.
Add the sliced shiitake mushrooms to the broth and let them simmer for about 2-3 minutes until softened.
Meanwhile, cook the ramen noodles according to package instructions. Drain and set aside.
Once the mushrooms are tender, add the baby spinach leaves to the broth. Let them wilt for about 1-2 minutes.
Divide the cooked ramen noodles into serving bowls.
Ladle the hot and spicy broth over the noodles in each bowl.
Top each bowl with the cooked tofu cubes.

Garnish with sliced green onions and sesame seeds.
Optionally, add a soft-boiled egg and sliced chili pepper for extra flavor and heat.
Serve hot and enjoy your Spicy Tofu Ramen with Sriracha!

This recipe offers a perfect balance of heat, spice, and savory flavors, making it a satisfying meal for any spicy food lover. Feel free to adjust the spiciness level by adding more or less Sriracha sauce.

Curry Laksa Ramen

Ingredients:

- 2 packs of ramen noodles (about 200g)
- 4 cups chicken or vegetable broth
- 1 can (14 oz) coconut milk
- 2 tablespoons curry powder
- 1 tablespoon chili paste or sambal oelek (adjust to taste)
- 2 tablespoons soy sauce
- 1 tablespoon brown sugar
- 1 tablespoon fish sauce (optional, for added depth of flavor)
- 1 tablespoon sesame oil
- 2 cloves garlic, minced
- 1 tablespoon grated ginger
- 2 cups cooked chicken, shredded (optional)
- 1 cup sliced tofu puffs or fried tofu cubes
- 1 cup bean sprouts
- 1 cup sliced shiitake mushrooms
- 2 green onions, thinly sliced
- Fresh cilantro leaves for garnish
- Lime wedges for serving

Instructions:

In a large pot, heat sesame oil over medium heat. Add minced garlic and grated ginger, and cook for about 1 minute until fragrant.

Stir in curry powder and chili paste (or sambal oelek) and cook for another minute to toast the spices.

Pour in the chicken or vegetable broth and bring it to a simmer.

Stir in coconut milk, soy sauce, brown sugar, and fish sauce (if using). Let the broth simmer for about 5-10 minutes to allow the flavors to meld.

Meanwhile, cook the ramen noodles according to package instructions. Drain and set aside.

Once the broth is ready, add the sliced shiitake mushrooms, cooked chicken (if using), tofu puffs, and bean sprouts. Let them simmer for about 2-3 minutes until heated through.

Divide the cooked ramen noodles into serving bowls.

Ladle the hot curry laksa broth over the noodles in each bowl.
Garnish each bowl with sliced green onions and fresh cilantro leaves.
Serve hot with lime wedges on the side for squeezing over the ramen.

Enjoy your flavorful and aromatic Curry Laksa Ramen! Feel free to customize it with your favorite protein and vegetables. Adjust the level of spiciness according to your taste preference by adding more or less chili paste.

Creamy Mushroom Ramen

Ingredients:

- 2 packs of ramen noodles (about 200g)
- 4 cups vegetable or chicken broth
- 2 tablespoons unsalted butter
- 1 onion, finely chopped
- 3 cloves garlic, minced
- 8 oz (about 225g) mixed mushrooms (such as shiitake, cremini, and oyster), sliced
- 1 teaspoon dried thyme
- 1 teaspoon dried rosemary
- Salt and pepper to taste
- 1 cup heavy cream
- 1/4 cup grated Parmesan cheese (optional)
- 2 green onions, thinly sliced (for garnish)
- Fresh parsley, chopped (for garnish)

Instructions:

Cook the ramen noodles according to package instructions. Drain and set aside.
In a large pot, melt the butter over medium heat. Add the chopped onion and cook until softened, about 3-4 minutes.
Add the minced garlic to the pot and cook for an additional minute until fragrant.
Add the sliced mushrooms to the pot and cook until they are tender and golden brown, about 5-6 minutes.
Stir in the dried thyme and rosemary, and season with salt and pepper to taste.
Pour in the vegetable or chicken broth and bring the mixture to a simmer. Let it simmer for about 10 minutes to allow the flavors to meld.
Stir in the heavy cream and grated Parmesan cheese (if using). Let the mixture simmer for an additional 5 minutes.
Divide the cooked ramen noodles into serving bowls.
Ladle the creamy mushroom broth over the noodles in each bowl.
Garnish each bowl with thinly sliced green onions and chopped fresh parsley.
Serve hot and enjoy your Creamy Mushroom Ramen!

This recipe provides a rich and creamy broth packed with the earthy flavors of mushrooms. Feel free to customize it by adding other vegetables or protein sources such as tofu or shredded chicken. Adjust the seasoning according to your taste preference.

Korean Jjajangmyeon Ramen

Ingredients:

- 2 packs of ramen noodles (about 200g)
- 1 tablespoon vegetable oil
- 1 onion, finely chopped
- 2 cloves garlic, minced
- 1 small zucchini, diced
- 1 small carrot, diced
- 1/2 cup diced potato
- 1/2 cup diced tofu or pork (optional)
- 2 tablespoons Korean black bean paste (Jjajang)
- 1 tablespoon soy sauce
- 1 tablespoon oyster sauce
- 1 teaspoon sugar
- 2 cups vegetable or chicken broth
- 1 tablespoon cornstarch mixed with 2 tablespoons water (optional, for thickening)
- Sliced cucumber for garnish
- Sliced green onions for garnish

Instructions:

Cook the ramen noodles according to package instructions. Drain and set aside.
In a large skillet or wok, heat the vegetable oil over medium heat.
Add the chopped onion and minced garlic to the skillet. Cook until the onion is translucent and fragrant, about 2-3 minutes.
Add the diced zucchini, carrot, potato, and tofu or pork (if using) to the skillet.
Cook for another 5 minutes until the vegetables are slightly softened.
Stir in the Korean black bean paste (Jjajang), soy sauce, oyster sauce, and sugar.
Cook for 2-3 minutes until the vegetables are well coated with the sauce.
Pour in the vegetable or chicken broth and bring the mixture to a simmer. Let it simmer for about 10 minutes to allow the flavors to meld.
If you prefer a thicker sauce, stir in the cornstarch mixture and cook for an additional 1-2 minutes until the sauce thickens.
Divide the cooked ramen noodles into serving bowls.
Ladle the Jjajang sauce and vegetables over the noodles in each bowl.

Garnish each bowl with sliced cucumber and green onions.
Serve hot and enjoy your Korean Jjajangmyeon Ramen!

This recipe offers a flavorful and satisfying take on the traditional Korean Jjajangmyeon dish, incorporating ramen noodles for added comfort. Feel free to customize it by adding your favorite vegetables or protein options. Adjust the seasoning according to your taste preference, and enjoy this delicious Korean-inspired ramen!

Duck Ramen with Hoisin Sauce

Ingredients:

- 2 duck breasts
- 2 packs of ramen noodles (about 200g)
- 4 cups chicken or vegetable broth
- 2 tablespoons hoisin sauce
- 1 tablespoon soy sauce
- 1 tablespoon rice vinegar
- 1 tablespoon sesame oil
- 2 cloves garlic, minced
- 1 tablespoon grated ginger
- 2 cups baby spinach leaves
- 1 cup sliced shiitake mushrooms
- 2 green onions, thinly sliced
- Sesame seeds for garnish
- Sliced chili pepper for garnish (optional)

Instructions:

Score the skin of the duck breasts and season them with salt and pepper.
Heat a skillet over medium-high heat. Place the duck breasts skin side down in the skillet and cook for about 6-8 minutes until the skin is crispy and golden brown. Flip the duck breasts and cook for an additional 3-4 minutes until cooked to your desired doneness. Remove the duck breasts from the skillet and let them rest for a few minutes before slicing thinly.
In a pot, bring the chicken or vegetable broth to a simmer over medium heat.
Stir in hoisin sauce, soy sauce, rice vinegar, sesame oil, minced garlic, and grated ginger. Let the broth simmer for about 5 minutes to allow the flavors to meld.
Cook the ramen noodles according to package instructions. Drain and set aside.
Once the broth is ready, add the baby spinach leaves and sliced shiitake mushrooms to the pot. Let them simmer for about 2-3 minutes until the vegetables are tender.
Divide the cooked ramen noodles into serving bowls.
Ladle the hot broth and vegetables over the noodles in each bowl.
Top each bowl with thinly sliced duck breast.
Garnish each bowl with sliced green onions and sesame seeds.

Optionally, add sliced chili pepper for extra heat.
Serve hot and enjoy your Duck Ramen with Hoisin Sauce!

This recipe offers a rich and savory broth with tender duck slices, complemented by the sweetness and depth of flavor from the hoisin sauce. Adjust the level of spiciness according to your taste preference.

Thai Peanut Ramen

Ingredients:

- 2 packs of ramen noodles (about 200g)
- 4 cups vegetable or chicken broth
- 1/4 cup creamy peanut butter
- 2 tablespoons soy sauce
- 2 tablespoons lime juice
- 2 tablespoons brown sugar
- 1 tablespoon grated ginger
- 2 cloves garlic, minced
- 1 tablespoon sesame oil
- 1 red bell pepper, thinly sliced
- 1 carrot, julienned or thinly sliced
- 1 cup shredded cabbage
- 1/2 cup sliced mushrooms (shiitake or button mushrooms)
- 1/4 cup chopped cilantro
- 1/4 cup chopped peanuts (for garnish)
- Lime wedges for serving

Instructions:

Cook the ramen noodles according to package instructions. Drain and set aside.
In a large pot, heat sesame oil over medium heat. Add minced garlic and grated ginger, and cook for about 1 minute until fragrant.
Pour in the vegetable or chicken broth and bring it to a simmer.
In a small bowl, whisk together peanut butter, soy sauce, lime juice, and brown sugar until smooth.
Stir the peanut butter mixture into the simmering broth. Let it simmer for about 5 minutes, stirring occasionally, to allow the flavors to meld.
Add the sliced red bell pepper, julienned carrot, shredded cabbage, and sliced mushrooms to the pot. Let them simmer for about 3-4 minutes until tender-crisp.
Divide the cooked ramen noodles into serving bowls.
Ladle the hot peanut broth and vegetables over the noodles in each bowl.
Garnish each bowl with chopped cilantro and chopped peanuts.
Serve hot with lime wedges on the side for squeezing over the ramen.

Enjoy your Thai Peanut Ramen! This dish offers a creamy and nutty broth with a burst of Thai-inspired flavors. Adjust the ingredients and seasonings according to your taste preference.

Spicy Tuna Ramen

Ingredients:

- 2 packs of ramen noodles (about 200g)
- 4 cups water
- 2 (5 oz) cans of tuna in water, drained
- 2 tablespoons soy sauce
- 1 tablespoon sesame oil
- 2 cloves garlic, minced
- 1 tablespoon grated ginger
- 2 tablespoons sriracha sauce (adjust to taste)
- 1 tablespoon rice vinegar
- 2 cups chopped bok choy or spinach
- 1/2 cup sliced shiitake mushrooms
- 2 green onions, thinly sliced
- Optional toppings: sliced boiled egg, nori seaweed, sesame seeds, sliced chili pepper

Instructions:

Cook the ramen noodles according to package instructions. Drain and set aside.
In a pot, bring water to a boil. Add minced garlic and grated ginger.
Stir in soy sauce, sesame oil, sriracha sauce, and rice vinegar.
Add the chopped bok choy or spinach and sliced shiitake mushrooms to the pot. Let them cook for about 2-3 minutes until slightly softened.
Add the drained tuna to the pot and stir to combine. Let it heat through for about 1-2 minutes.
Divide the cooked ramen noodles into serving bowls.
Ladle the spicy tuna broth and vegetables over the noodles in each bowl.
Garnish each bowl with sliced green onions and any optional toppings you desire.
Serve hot and enjoy your Spicy Tuna Ramen!

Feel free to adjust the level of spiciness by adding more or less sriracha sauce according to your taste preference. You can also customize the toppings based on your liking.

Pork Ramen with Kimchi and Egg

Ingredients:

- 2 packs of ramen noodles (about 200g)
- 4 cups chicken or pork broth
- 2 cups thinly sliced pork belly or pork shoulder
- 2 tablespoons soy sauce
- 1 tablespoon sesame oil
- 2 cloves garlic, minced
- 1 tablespoon grated ginger
- 1 cup kimchi, chopped
- 4 large eggs
- 2 cups chopped bok choy or spinach
- 2 green onions, thinly sliced
- Sesame seeds for garnish
- Optional: Sriracha or chili oil for extra heat

Instructions:

In a pot, bring the chicken or pork broth to a simmer over medium heat.
In a separate skillet, heat the sesame oil over medium-high heat. Add the thinly sliced pork belly or pork shoulder and cook until browned and cooked through.
Add minced garlic and grated ginger to the skillet with the pork and cook for another minute until fragrant.
Stir in soy sauce and continue to cook for another minute. Remove from heat and set aside.
Meanwhile, bring a separate pot of water to a boil. Carefully add the eggs and boil for about 7 minutes for soft-boiled eggs or longer for hard-boiled eggs. Once done, transfer the eggs to a bowl of ice water to stop the cooking process. Peel the eggs and set them aside.
Add the chopped kimchi and chopped bok choy or spinach to the simmering broth. Let them cook for about 2-3 minutes until softened.
Cook the ramen noodles according to package instructions. Drain and divide them into serving bowls.
Ladle the hot broth with kimchi and vegetables over the noodles in each bowl.
Top each bowl with slices of cooked pork.
Halve the boiled eggs and place one half in each bowl.

Garnish each bowl with sliced green onions and sesame seeds.
Optionally, add a drizzle of Sriracha or chili oil for extra heat.
Serve hot and enjoy your Pork Ramen with Kimchi and Egg!

This recipe offers a delicious combination of tender pork, flavorful broth, tangy kimchi, and creamy egg, creating a hearty and satisfying meal. Adjust the level of spiciness and customize the toppings according to your taste preference.

Coconut Lime Chicken Ramen

Ingredients:

- 2 packs of ramen noodles (about 200g)
- 4 cups chicken broth
- 1 can (14 oz) coconut milk
- 2 tablespoons fish sauce
- 2 tablespoons soy sauce
- 2 tablespoons lime juice
- Zest of 1 lime
- 1 tablespoon brown sugar
- 2 cloves garlic, minced
- 1 tablespoon grated ginger
- 2 boneless, skinless chicken breasts, thinly sliced
- 1 red bell pepper, thinly sliced
- 1 cup sliced shiitake mushrooms
- 2 green onions, thinly sliced
- Fresh cilantro leaves for garnish
- Sliced chili pepper for garnish (optional)

Instructions:

In a large pot, combine chicken broth, coconut milk, fish sauce, soy sauce, lime juice, lime zest, and brown sugar. Stir well to combine.

Add minced garlic and grated ginger to the pot. Bring the mixture to a simmer over medium heat.

Add thinly sliced chicken breasts to the pot and let them cook for about 5-7 minutes until cooked through.

Stir in sliced red bell pepper and sliced shiitake mushrooms. Let them simmer for an additional 3-4 minutes until the vegetables are tender.

While the soup is simmering, cook the ramen noodles according to package instructions. Drain and set aside.

Divide the cooked ramen noodles into serving bowls.

Ladle the hot coconut lime chicken broth and vegetables over the noodles in each bowl.

Garnish each bowl with sliced green onions, fresh cilantro leaves, and sliced chili pepper (if using).

Serve hot and enjoy your Coconut Lime Chicken Ramen!

This recipe offers a delightful combination of creamy coconut milk, tangy lime, and savory chicken, creating a flavorful and aromatic broth. Adjust the level of spiciness by adding sliced chili pepper according to your taste preference.

Japanese Curry Ramen

Ingredients:

- 2 packs of ramen noodles (about 200g)
- 4 cups chicken or vegetable broth
- 2 tablespoons Japanese curry roux (store-bought or homemade)
- 1 tablespoon soy sauce
- 1 tablespoon mirin (Japanese sweet rice wine)
- 1 tablespoon sesame oil
- 2 cloves garlic, minced
- 1 tablespoon grated ginger
- 2 cups chopped vegetables (carrots, potatoes, onions)
- 2 cups cooked protein (sliced chicken, pork, beef, tofu)
- 2 boiled eggs, halved
- Sliced green onions for garnish
- Toasted sesame seeds for garnish

Instructions:

In a large pot, heat sesame oil over medium heat. Add minced garlic and grated ginger, and cook for about 1 minute until fragrant.
Add chopped vegetables to the pot and sauté for a few minutes until they start to soften.
Pour in the chicken or vegetable broth and bring it to a simmer.
Stir in Japanese curry roux, soy sauce, and mirin. Let the curry simmer for about 10-15 minutes until the vegetables are tender and the curry thickens.
Meanwhile, cook the ramen noodles according to package instructions. Drain and set aside.
Once the curry is ready, divide the cooked ramen noodles into serving bowls.
Ladle the hot Japanese curry broth and vegetables over the noodles in each bowl.
Add slices of cooked protein (chicken, pork, beef, tofu) to each bowl.
Top each bowl with a halved boiled egg.
Garnish each bowl with sliced green onions and toasted sesame seeds.
Serve hot and enjoy your Japanese Curry Ramen!

This recipe offers a comforting and flavorful bowl of ramen with the aromatic spices of Japanese curry. Feel free to customize it with your favorite vegetables and protein options. Adjust the seasoning according to your taste preference.

Vegetarian Ramen with Crispy Tofu

Ingredients:

- 2 packs of ramen noodles (about 200g)
- 4 cups vegetable broth
- 1 block (about 14 oz) extra-firm tofu, pressed and cubed
- 2 tablespoons soy sauce
- 1 tablespoon sesame oil
- 2 cloves garlic, minced
- 1 tablespoon grated ginger
- 2 cups sliced shiitake mushrooms
- 1 cup sliced carrots
- 2 cups baby spinach leaves
- 2 green onions, thinly sliced
- Sesame seeds for garnish
- Optional toppings: sliced boiled egg, nori seaweed, sliced chili pepper

Instructions:

Preheat your oven to 400°F (200°C). Line a baking sheet with parchment paper.
In a bowl, combine cubed tofu, soy sauce, and sesame oil. Toss to coat the tofu evenly.
Spread the tofu cubes in a single layer on the prepared baking sheet. Bake for 25-30 minutes, flipping halfway through, until the tofu is crispy and golden brown.
In a large pot, heat some oil over medium heat. Add minced garlic and grated ginger, and cook for about 1 minute until fragrant.
Pour in the vegetable broth and bring it to a simmer.
Add sliced shiitake mushrooms and sliced carrots to the pot. Let them simmer for about 5-7 minutes until tender.
Cook the ramen noodles according to package instructions. Drain and set aside.
Once the vegetables are tender, add the baby spinach leaves to the pot. Let them wilt for about 1-2 minutes.
Divide the cooked ramen noodles into serving bowls.
Ladle the hot broth and vegetables over the noodles in each bowl.
Top each bowl with crispy tofu cubes.
Garnish each bowl with sliced green onions and sesame seeds.

Optionally, add additional toppings like sliced boiled egg, nori seaweed, or sliced chili pepper for extra flavor and texture.
Serve hot and enjoy your Vegetarian Ramen with Crispy Tofu!

This recipe offers a delicious and nutritious vegetarian ramen option with crispy tofu as the protein source. Feel free to customize it with your favorite vegetables and toppings. Adjust the seasoning according to your taste preference.

Beef Bulgogi Ramen

Ingredients:

- 2 packs of ramen noodles (about 200g)
- 1 lb (450g) beef sirloin or ribeye, thinly sliced
- 4 cups beef broth
- 1/4 cup soy sauce
- 2 tablespoons brown sugar
- 2 tablespoons sesame oil
- 4 cloves garlic, minced
- 1 tablespoon grated ginger
- 1 onion, thinly sliced
- 1 carrot, julienned
- 2 cups sliced mushrooms (shiitake or button mushrooms)
- 2 cups baby spinach leaves
- 2 green onions, thinly sliced
- Sesame seeds for garnish
- Optional toppings: sliced boiled egg, kimchi

Instructions:

In a bowl, combine soy sauce, brown sugar, sesame oil, minced garlic, and grated ginger. Add the thinly sliced beef and toss to coat. Let marinate for at least 30 minutes, or ideally overnight in the refrigerator.

In a large pot, bring the beef broth to a simmer over medium heat.

Add marinated beef slices to the pot and let them cook for about 2-3 minutes until browned.

Add sliced onion, julienned carrot, and sliced mushrooms to the pot. Let them simmer for about 5 minutes until the vegetables are tender.

Meanwhile, cook the ramen noodles according to package instructions. Drain and set aside.

Once the vegetables are tender, add baby spinach leaves to the pot. Let them wilt for about 1-2 minutes.

Divide the cooked ramen noodles into serving bowls.

Ladle the hot beef bulgogi broth and vegetables over the noodles in each bowl.

Garnish each bowl with sliced green onions and sesame seeds.

Optionally, add sliced boiled egg and kimchi as toppings for extra flavor and texture.
Serve hot and enjoy your Beef Bulgogi Ramen!

This recipe offers a delicious fusion of Korean bulgogi flavors with the comforting warmth of ramen noodles. Adjust the seasoning according to your taste preference and feel free to customize it with your favorite toppings.

Creamy Pesto Ramen

Ingredients:

- 2 packs of ramen noodles (about 200g)
- 2 cups fresh basil leaves
- 1/4 cup pine nuts
- 2 cloves garlic
- 1/4 cup grated Parmesan cheese
- 1/4 cup olive oil
- Salt and pepper to taste
- 4 cups vegetable or chicken broth
- 1 cup heavy cream
- 2 tablespoons unsalted butter
- 1 tablespoon olive oil
- 2 cloves garlic, minced
- 1 cup sliced mushrooms
- 1 cup cherry tomatoes, halved
- 2 cups baby spinach leaves
- Salt and pepper to taste
- Grated Parmesan cheese for garnish

Instructions:

In a food processor, combine fresh basil leaves, pine nuts, garlic, grated Parmesan cheese, and olive oil. Pulse until smooth. Season with salt and pepper to taste. Set aside.

In a large pot, bring the vegetable or chicken broth to a simmer over medium heat.

Cook the ramen noodles according to package instructions. Drain and set aside.

In a separate skillet, heat unsalted butter and olive oil over medium heat. Add minced garlic and cook until fragrant, about 1 minute.

Add sliced mushrooms to the skillet and cook until they are tender and golden brown, about 5-7 minutes.

Stir in halved cherry tomatoes and cook for an additional 2-3 minutes until softened.

Pour the creamy pesto sauce into the simmering broth. Stir in heavy cream and let it simmer for about 5 minutes to allow the flavors to meld.

Add baby spinach leaves to the pot and let them wilt for about 1-2 minutes.
Season the broth with salt and pepper to taste.
Divide the cooked ramen noodles into serving bowls.
Ladle the hot creamy pesto broth and vegetables over the noodles in each bowl.
Garnish each bowl with grated Parmesan cheese.
Serve hot and enjoy your Creamy Pesto Ramen!

This recipe offers a deliciously creamy and flavorful twist on traditional ramen, perfect for pesto lovers. Adjust the seasoning and consistency of the pesto sauce according to your taste preference. Enjoy the rich and comforting flavors of this unique dish!

Mexican Ramen with Black Beans and Avocado

Ingredients:

- 2 packs of ramen noodles (about 200g)
- 4 cups vegetable or chicken broth
- 1 can (15 oz) black beans, drained and rinsed
- 1 tablespoon olive oil
- 1 onion, diced
- 2 cloves garlic, minced
- 1 bell pepper, diced
- 1 jalapeño pepper, seeded and diced (optional, for extra heat)
- 1 teaspoon ground cumin
- 1 teaspoon chili powder
- 1/2 teaspoon smoked paprika
- Salt and pepper to taste
- 1 avocado, diced
- 1/4 cup chopped fresh cilantro
- Lime wedges for serving
- Optional toppings: shredded cheese, sour cream, diced tomatoes, sliced green onions

Instructions:

Cook the ramen noodles according to package instructions. Drain and set aside.
In a large pot, heat olive oil over medium heat. Add diced onion and cook until softened, about 3-4 minutes.
Add minced garlic, diced bell pepper, and diced jalapeño pepper (if using) to the pot. Cook for another 2-3 minutes until the vegetables are tender.
Stir in ground cumin, chili powder, smoked paprika, salt, and pepper. Cook for another minute to toast the spices.
Pour in the vegetable or chicken broth and bring it to a simmer.
Add drained and rinsed black beans to the pot. Let the mixture simmer for about 10-15 minutes to allow the flavors to meld.
Divide the cooked ramen noodles into serving bowls.
Ladle the hot Mexican-style broth and vegetables over the noodles in each bowl.
Top each bowl with diced avocado and chopped fresh cilantro.
Serve hot with lime wedges on the side for squeezing over the ramen.

Optionally, garnish each bowl with shredded cheese, sour cream, diced tomatoes, and sliced green onions for extra flavor and texture.
Enjoy your Mexican Ramen with Black Beans and Avocado!

This recipe offers a delicious and satisfying twist on traditional ramen, with the bold flavors of Mexican spices, hearty black beans, creamy avocado, and fresh cilantro. Feel free to customize it with your favorite toppings and adjust the level of spiciness according to your taste preference.

Lemongrass Chicken Ramen

Ingredients:

- 2 packs of ramen noodles (about 200g)
- 4 cups chicken broth
- 2 lemongrass stalks, outer layers removed and smashed
- 2 boneless, skinless chicken breasts, thinly sliced
- 2 tablespoons soy sauce
- 1 tablespoon fish sauce
- 1 tablespoon lime juice
- 1 tablespoon brown sugar
- 1 tablespoon sesame oil
- 2 cloves garlic, minced
- 1 tablespoon grated ginger
- 1 red chili pepper, sliced (optional, for extra heat)
- 2 cups sliced vegetables (such as bell peppers, carrots, mushrooms)
- 2 cups baby spinach leaves
- 2 green onions, thinly sliced
- Fresh cilantro leaves for garnish
- Lime wedges for serving

Instructions:

In a large pot, bring the chicken broth to a simmer over medium heat.
Add smashed lemongrass stalks to the pot and let them simmer for about 5 minutes to infuse the broth with flavor. Remove and discard the lemongrass.
In a bowl, combine thinly sliced chicken breasts, soy sauce, fish sauce, lime juice, brown sugar, minced garlic, and grated ginger. Let the chicken marinate for about 15-20 minutes.
In a separate skillet or wok, heat sesame oil over medium-high heat. Add the marinated chicken slices (reserve the marinade) and cook until they are browned and cooked through, about 5-6 minutes.
Remove the cooked chicken from the skillet and set aside.
In the same skillet, add sliced vegetables and cook for about 3-4 minutes until they are tender-crisp.
Pour the reserved marinade into the skillet with the vegetables and let it cook for another minute.

Meanwhile, cook the ramen noodles according to package instructions. Drain and set aside.

Once the vegetables are cooked, add baby spinach leaves to the skillet and let them wilt for about 1-2 minutes.

Divide the cooked ramen noodles into serving bowls.

Ladle the hot lemongrass-infused chicken broth over the noodles in each bowl.

Top each bowl with cooked chicken slices and sautéed vegetables.

Garnish each bowl with sliced green onions, fresh cilantro leaves, and sliced red chili pepper (if using).

Serve hot with lime wedges on the side for squeezing over the ramen.

This Lemongrass Chicken Ramen offers a refreshing and aromatic twist on traditional ramen, perfect for a comforting and satisfying meal. Adjust the level of spiciness by adding more or less red chili pepper according to your taste preference. Enjoy!

Teriyaki Salmon Ramen

Ingredients:

- 2 packs of ramen noodles (about 200g)
- 2 salmon fillets (about 6 oz each), skin removed
- 1/4 cup teriyaki sauce
- 4 cups vegetable or chicken broth
- 2 tablespoons soy sauce
- 1 tablespoon mirin (Japanese sweet rice wine)
- 1 tablespoon sesame oil
- 2 cloves garlic, minced
- 1 tablespoon grated ginger
- 2 cups chopped vegetables (such as bok choy, spinach, carrots)
- 2 green onions, thinly sliced
- Sesame seeds for garnish
- Optional toppings: sliced boiled egg, nori seaweed, sliced chili pepper

Instructions:

Preheat your oven to 400°F (200°C). Line a baking sheet with parchment paper.
Place the salmon fillets on the prepared baking sheet and brush them with teriyaki sauce, coating them evenly.
Bake the salmon in the preheated oven for about 12-15 minutes, or until cooked through and flaky.
Meanwhile, in a large pot, bring the vegetable or chicken broth to a simmer over medium heat.
Add soy sauce, mirin, sesame oil, minced garlic, and grated ginger to the pot. Stir well to combine.
Add chopped vegetables to the pot and let them simmer for about 5-7 minutes until tender.
Cook the ramen noodles according to package instructions. Drain and set aside.
Once the vegetables are tender, divide the cooked ramen noodles into serving bowls.
Ladle the hot broth and vegetables over the noodles in each bowl.
Place a teriyaki-glazed salmon fillet on top of the noodles in each bowl.
Garnish each bowl with sliced green onions and sesame seeds.
Optionally, add sliced boiled egg and nori seaweed as toppings for extra flavor and texture.

Serve hot and enjoy your Teriyaki Salmon Ramen!

This recipe offers a delightful combination of tender salmon, savory broth, and flavorful vegetables, all served over comforting ramen noodles. Customize it with your favorite toppings and adjust the seasoning according to your taste preference. Enjoy!

Italian Sausage Ramen

Ingredients:

- 2 packs of ramen noodles (about 200g)
- 4 cups chicken or vegetable broth
- 2 Italian sausage links, casings removed
- 1 tablespoon olive oil
- 1 onion, diced
- 2 cloves garlic, minced
- 1 bell pepper, diced
- 1 can (14 oz) diced tomatoes
- 1 teaspoon Italian seasoning
- Salt and pepper to taste
- 2 cups baby spinach leaves
- Grated Parmesan cheese for garnish
- Fresh basil leaves for garnish

Instructions:

In a large pot, heat olive oil over medium heat. Add the Italian sausage, breaking it up with a spoon, and cook until browned and cooked through.

Add diced onion and minced garlic to the pot. Cook for about 2-3 minutes until the onion is softened and translucent.

Stir in diced bell pepper and cook for another 2-3 minutes until the pepper is softened.

Add diced tomatoes (with their juices) to the pot. Stir in Italian seasoning, salt, and pepper.

Pour in the chicken or vegetable broth and bring it to a simmer.

Meanwhile, cook the ramen noodles according to package instructions. Drain and set aside.

Once the broth is simmering and the vegetables are tender, add baby spinach leaves to the pot. Let them wilt for about 1-2 minutes.

Divide the cooked ramen noodles into serving bowls.

Ladle the hot Italian sausage broth and vegetables over the noodles in each bowl.

Garnish each bowl with grated Parmesan cheese and fresh basil leaves.

Serve hot and enjoy your Italian Sausage Ramen!

This recipe offers a flavorful and satisfying twist on traditional ramen, with the savory goodness of Italian sausage and the richness of tomatoes and spices. Adjust the seasoning according to your taste preference and garnish with your favorite herbs and cheese. Enjoy!

Vegetable Ramen Stir-Fry

Ingredients:

- 2 packs of ramen noodles (about 200g)
- 2 tablespoons vegetable oil
- 2 cloves garlic, minced
- 1 tablespoon grated ginger
- 1 onion, thinly sliced
- 1 bell pepper, thinly sliced
- 2 cups sliced mushrooms (shiitake, button, or your choice)
- 1 carrot, julienned or thinly sliced
- 2 cups shredded cabbage or coleslaw mix
- 1 cup snow peas or sugar snap peas, trimmed
- 1/4 cup soy sauce
- 2 tablespoons oyster sauce (optional)
- 1 tablespoon rice vinegar
- 1 teaspoon sesame oil
- Salt and pepper to taste
- Sesame seeds and sliced green onions for garnish

Instructions:

Cook the ramen noodles according to package instructions. Drain and set aside.
In a large skillet or wok, heat vegetable oil over medium-high heat.
Add minced garlic and grated ginger to the skillet. Stir-fry for about 30 seconds until fragrant.
Add thinly sliced onion, bell pepper, mushrooms, and julienned carrot to the skillet. Stir-fry for about 3-4 minutes until the vegetables are slightly softened.
Add shredded cabbage and snow peas to the skillet. Continue to stir-fry for another 2-3 minutes until the cabbage is wilted and the snow peas are tender-crisp.
In a small bowl, mix together soy sauce, oyster sauce (if using), rice vinegar, and sesame oil.
Pour the sauce mixture over the vegetables in the skillet. Stir to coat evenly.
Add the cooked ramen noodles to the skillet. Toss everything together until the noodles are well coated with the sauce and heated through.
Season with salt and pepper to taste.

Remove from heat and transfer the Vegetable Ramen Stir-Fry to serving plates or bowls.
Garnish with sesame seeds and sliced green onions.
Serve hot and enjoy your Vegetable Ramen Stir-Fry!

Feel free to customize this recipe by adding your favorite vegetables or protein options such as tofu, tempeh, or cooked chicken or shrimp. Adjust the seasoning and sauce according to your taste preference. It's a versatile and delicious dish that's perfect for a quick and satisfying meal.

Chipotle Chicken Ramen

Ingredients:

- 2 packs of ramen noodles (about 200g)
- 4 cups chicken broth
- 2 boneless, skinless chicken breasts, thinly sliced
- 2 chipotle peppers in adobo sauce, finely chopped
- 2 tablespoons adobo sauce (from the chipotle pepper can)
- 2 tablespoons olive oil
- 1 onion, finely chopped
- 3 cloves garlic, minced
- 1 red bell pepper, thinly sliced
- 1 cup corn kernels (fresh, canned, or frozen)
- 2 cups baby spinach leaves
- Salt and pepper to taste
- Lime wedges for serving
- Fresh cilantro leaves for garnish
- Sliced avocado for garnish
- Sour cream or Greek yogurt for garnish (optional)

Instructions:

In a large pot, heat olive oil over medium heat. Add chopped onion and cook until softened, about 3-4 minutes.

Add minced garlic and chopped chipotle peppers to the pot. Cook for another minute until fragrant.

Stir in adobo sauce and sliced red bell pepper. Cook for about 2-3 minutes until the pepper starts to soften.

Add thinly sliced chicken breasts to the pot. Cook until the chicken is no longer pink and cooked through, about 5-7 minutes.

Pour in chicken broth and bring it to a simmer.

Meanwhile, cook the ramen noodles according to package instructions. Drain and set aside.

Once the chicken is cooked and the broth is simmering, add corn kernels and baby spinach leaves to the pot. Let them cook for about 2-3 minutes until the spinach wilts and the corn is heated through.

Season the broth with salt and pepper to taste.

Divide the cooked ramen noodles into serving bowls.
Ladle the hot chipotle chicken broth and vegetables over the noodles in each bowl.
Garnish each bowl with fresh cilantro leaves and sliced avocado.
Serve hot with lime wedges on the side for squeezing over the ramen.
Optionally, add a dollop of sour cream or Greek yogurt for extra creaminess.

Enjoy your Chipotle Chicken Ramen! This dish offers a delightful blend of smoky

chipotle flavor, tender chicken, and comforting noodles, perfect for a satisfying meal.

Adjust the spiciness according to your taste preference.

Shrimp Tempura Ramen

Ingredients:

For Shrimp Tempura:

- 12 large shrimp, peeled and deveined
- 1 cup all-purpose flour
- 1 cup cold water
- 1 egg
- 1 teaspoon baking powder
- Vegetable oil for frying
- Salt to taste

For Ramen:

- 2 packs of ramen noodles (about 200g)
- 4 cups chicken or vegetable broth
- 2 cups water
- 2 tablespoons soy sauce
- 1 tablespoon mirin (Japanese sweet rice wine)
- 1 tablespoon sesame oil
- 2 cloves garlic, minced
- 1 tablespoon grated ginger
- 2 cups sliced mushrooms (shiitake or button mushrooms)
- 2 cups baby spinach leaves
- 2 green onions, thinly sliced
- Nori seaweed sheets, sliced (for garnish)
- Sesame seeds (for garnish)
- Optional toppings: sliced boiled egg, corn kernels, bamboo shoots, sliced chili pepper

Instructions:

For Shrimp Tempura:

In a bowl, whisk together all-purpose flour, cold water, egg, and baking powder until the batter is smooth. It should have a pancake batter-like consistency.
Heat vegetable oil in a deep fryer or large pot to 350°F (175°C).
Dip each shrimp into the batter, coating it completely.
Carefully place the battered shrimp into the hot oil and fry until golden brown and crispy, about 2-3 minutes per side. Fry in batches to avoid overcrowding the fryer.
Remove the shrimp from the oil using a slotted spoon and transfer them to a paper towel-lined plate to drain excess oil. Sprinkle with salt while still hot.

For Ramen:

In a large pot, combine chicken or vegetable broth, water, soy sauce, mirin, sesame oil, minced garlic, and grated ginger. Bring to a simmer over medium heat.
Add sliced mushrooms to the pot and let them simmer for about 3-4 minutes until softened.
Cook the ramen noodles according to package instructions. Drain and set aside.
Once the mushrooms are tender, add baby spinach leaves to the pot and let them wilt for about 1-2 minutes.
Divide the cooked ramen noodles into serving bowls.
Ladle the hot broth and vegetables over the noodles in each bowl.
Top each bowl with shrimp tempura, sliced green onions, nori seaweed sheets, and sesame seeds.
Optionally, add additional toppings like sliced boiled egg, corn kernels, bamboo shoots, or sliced chili pepper for extra flavor and texture.
Serve hot and enjoy your Shrimp Tempura Ramen!

This recipe offers a delicious and satisfying bowl of ramen with crispy shrimp tempura as the perfect complement to the flavorful broth and noodles. Adjust the toppings according to your taste preference. Enjoy!

Moroccan Spiced Lamb Ramen

Ingredients:

For the broth:

- 2 packs of ramen noodles (about 200g)
- 6 cups chicken or beef broth
- 1 onion, chopped
- 3 cloves garlic, minced
- 1 tablespoon grated fresh ginger
- 2 tablespoons tomato paste
- 2 teaspoons ground cumin
- 1 teaspoon ground coriander
- 1 teaspoon ground cinnamon
- 1/2 teaspoon ground turmeric
- 1/4 teaspoon ground cloves
- 1/4 teaspoon ground nutmeg
- 1/4 teaspoon cayenne pepper (adjust to taste)
- Salt and pepper to taste
- 2 tablespoons olive oil

For the lamb:

- 1 lb (450g) lamb leg or shoulder, thinly sliced
- 2 teaspoons ground cumin
- 1 teaspoon ground coriander
- 1 teaspoon smoked paprika
- 1/2 teaspoon ground cinnamon
- Salt and pepper to taste
- 2 tablespoons olive oil

For serving:

- Chopped fresh cilantro leaves
- Sliced green onions
- Lime wedges
- Sliced chili peppers (optional)

Instructions:

In a large pot, heat olive oil over medium heat. Add chopped onion and cook until softened, about 5 minutes. Add minced garlic and grated ginger, and cook for another minute until fragrant.

Stir in tomato paste and all the Moroccan spices (cumin, coriander, cinnamon, turmeric, cloves, nutmeg, cayenne pepper). Cook for a couple of minutes to toast the spices and develop their flavors.

Pour in the chicken or beef broth and bring the mixture to a simmer. Let it simmer for about 20-30 minutes to allow the flavors to meld. Season with salt and pepper to taste.

Meanwhile, prepare the lamb by mixing together the spices (cumin, coriander, smoked paprika, cinnamon, salt, and pepper) in a bowl. Rub the spice mixture all over the thinly sliced lamb.

Heat olive oil in a skillet over medium-high heat. Add the seasoned lamb slices and cook for about 2-3 minutes per side until browned and cooked to your desired doneness. Remove from the skillet and set aside.

Cook the ramen noodles according to package instructions. Drain and set aside.

To serve, divide the cooked ramen noodles into bowls. Ladle the Moroccan spiced broth over the noodles. Top each bowl with slices of cooked lamb.

Garnish each bowl with chopped fresh cilantro, sliced green onions, and lime wedges. Optionally, add sliced chili peppers for extra heat.

Serve hot and enjoy your Moroccan Spiced Lamb Ramen!

This recipe offers a unique and flavorful twist on traditional ramen, infusing it with the rich and aromatic spices of Moroccan cuisine. Adjust the spice levels according to your preference and enjoy the hearty and comforting flavors of this dish.

Thai Red Curry Ramen

Ingredients:

For the broth:

- 2 packs of ramen noodles (about 200g)
- 4 cups vegetable or chicken broth
- 2 tablespoons Thai red curry paste
- 1 can (14 oz) coconut milk
- 2 tablespoons soy sauce
- 1 tablespoon brown sugar
- 1 tablespoon lime juice
- 2 cloves garlic, minced
- 1 tablespoon grated ginger
- 1 tablespoon vegetable oil

For the toppings:

- 1 cup sliced bell peppers (red, green, or yellow)
- 1 cup sliced mushrooms (shiitake, button, or your choice)
- 1 cup thinly sliced carrots
- 1 cup baby spinach leaves
- 1 block (about 14 oz) extra-firm tofu, pressed and cubed
- Fresh cilantro leaves for garnish
- Lime wedges for serving
- Sliced red chili peppers for garnish (optional)

Instructions:

In a large pot, heat vegetable oil over medium heat. Add minced garlic and grated ginger, and cook for about 1 minute until fragrant.
Stir in Thai red curry paste and cook for another minute to release its flavors.
Pour in the vegetable or chicken broth and bring it to a simmer.
Stir in coconut milk, soy sauce, brown sugar, and lime juice. Let the broth simmer for about 10-15 minutes to allow the flavors to meld.

Meanwhile, prepare the toppings. In a separate skillet, heat a little oil over medium-high heat. Add sliced bell peppers, mushrooms, and carrots. Cook for about 5-7 minutes until the vegetables are tender-crisp.

Add baby spinach leaves to the skillet and let them wilt for about 1-2 minutes. Remove from heat and set aside.

In the same skillet, add cubed tofu and cook until golden brown on all sides, about 5-7 minutes. Remove from heat and set aside.

Cook the ramen noodles according to package instructions. Drain and set aside.

To serve, divide the cooked ramen noodles into serving bowls. Ladle the hot Thai red curry broth over the noodles in each bowl.

Top each bowl with the cooked vegetables and tofu.

Garnish each bowl with fresh cilantro leaves and sliced red chili peppers (if using). Serve hot with lime wedges on the side for squeezing over the ramen.

Enjoy your Thai Red Curry Ramen!

This recipe offers a delicious fusion of Thai flavors and comforting ramen noodles. Feel free to customize the toppings with your favorite vegetables and protein options. Adjust the spice levels according to your taste preference.

Vegan Ramen with Shiitake Mushrooms

Ingredients:

For the broth:

- 2 packs of ramen noodles (about 200g)
- 6 cups vegetable broth
- 1 onion, chopped
- 3 cloves garlic, minced
- 1 tablespoon grated ginger
- 4-5 dried shiitake mushrooms
- 2 tablespoons soy sauce
- 1 tablespoon miso paste
- 1 tablespoon rice vinegar
- 1 teaspoon sesame oil
- Salt and pepper to taste

For the toppings:

- 2 cups sliced fresh shiitake mushrooms
- 1 tablespoon vegetable oil
- 2 cups baby spinach leaves
- 2 green onions, thinly sliced
- Sesame seeds for garnish
- Nori seaweed sheets, sliced thinly (optional)

Instructions:

In a large pot, heat vegetable oil over medium heat. Add chopped onion, minced garlic, and grated ginger. Cook until softened and fragrant, about 5 minutes. Add vegetable broth to the pot along with dried shiitake mushrooms. Bring to a simmer and let it cook for about 15-20 minutes to infuse the flavors.
While the broth is simmering, prepare the fresh shiitake mushrooms. Heat vegetable oil in a skillet over medium-high heat. Add sliced shiitake mushrooms and cook until they are golden brown and crispy, about 5-7 minutes. Remove from heat and set aside.

Once the broth is flavored to your liking, remove the dried shiitake mushrooms and discard them. Stir in soy sauce, miso paste, rice vinegar, and sesame oil. Season with salt and pepper to taste.

Cook the ramen noodles according to package instructions. Drain and set aside.

To serve, divide the cooked ramen noodles into serving bowls. Ladle the hot broth over the noodles in each bowl.

Top each bowl with crispy shiitake mushrooms, fresh baby spinach leaves, and sliced green onions.

Garnish each bowl with sesame seeds and thinly sliced nori seaweed sheets if desired.

Serve hot and enjoy your Vegan Ramen with Shiitake Mushrooms!

This recipe offers a delicious and nutritious vegan ramen option that's packed with umami-rich flavors from the shiitake mushrooms and savory broth. Feel free to customize the toppings with your favorite vegetables and garnishes. Adjust the seasoning according to your taste preference.

Hawaiian Lomi Lomi Salmon Ramen

Ingredients:

For the Lomi Lomi Salmon:

- 1 lb (about 450g) fresh salmon fillet, skin removed
- 1 tomato, diced
- 1/2 onion, finely chopped
- 2 green onions, thinly sliced
- 1/4 cup chopped cilantro
- Juice of 1 lime
- 1 tablespoon soy sauce
- 1 tablespoon sesame oil
- Salt and pepper to taste

For the Ramen:

- 2 packs of ramen noodles (about 200g)
- 4 cups vegetable or chicken broth
- 1 tablespoon soy sauce
- 1 tablespoon mirin (Japanese sweet rice wine)
- 1 tablespoon sesame oil
- 2 cloves garlic, minced
- 1 tablespoon grated ginger
- 2 cups chopped vegetables (such as bok choy, spinach, carrots)
- 1 cup sliced mushrooms (shiitake, button, or your choice)
- Optional toppings: sliced green onions, sesame seeds, nori seaweed sheets

Instructions:

Start by preparing the Lomi Lomi Salmon. Dice the salmon into small cubes and place them in a bowl.

Add diced tomato, finely chopped onion, thinly sliced green onions, chopped cilantro, lime juice, soy sauce, sesame oil, salt, and pepper to the bowl with the salmon. Gently toss to combine. Cover and refrigerate while you prepare the ramen.

In a large pot, bring the vegetable or chicken broth to a simmer over medium heat.

Stir in soy sauce, mirin, sesame oil, minced garlic, and grated ginger. Let the broth simmer for about 5 minutes to allow the flavors to meld.

Cook the ramen noodles according to package instructions. Drain and set aside.

Add chopped vegetables and sliced mushrooms to the pot with the broth. Let them simmer for about 3-5 minutes until tender.

To serve, divide the cooked ramen noodles into serving bowls.

Ladle the hot broth and vegetables over the noodles in each bowl.

Top each bowl with a generous portion of Lomi Lomi Salmon mixture.

Garnish each bowl with sliced green onions, sesame seeds, and torn nori seaweed sheets if desired.

Serve hot and enjoy your Hawaiian Lomi Lomi Salmon Ramen!

This recipe offers a delicious fusion of Hawaiian flavors with the comforting warmth of ramen noodles. The refreshing and vibrant Lomi Lomi Salmon adds a unique twist to traditional ramen. Adjust the seasoning according to your taste preference and enjoy this delightful dish!

Korean Spicy Beef Ramen

Ingredients:

For the spicy beef:

- 1 lb (about 450g) beef sirloin or flank steak, thinly sliced
- 2 tablespoons soy sauce
- 1 tablespoon gochujang (Korean red chili paste)
- 1 tablespoon sesame oil
- 2 cloves garlic, minced
- 1 tablespoon brown sugar
- 1 teaspoon grated ginger
- 1 tablespoon vegetable oil

For the ramen:

- 2 packs of ramen noodles (about 200g)
- 4 cups beef broth
- 2 tablespoons gochujang (Korean red chili paste)
- 2 tablespoons soy sauce
- 2 tablespoons sesame oil
- 2 cloves garlic, minced
- 1 tablespoon grated ginger
- 2 cups chopped vegetables (such as bok choy, spinach, carrots)
- 2 green onions, thinly sliced
- Optional toppings: sliced boiled egg, sliced kimchi, sesame seeds

Instructions:

In a bowl, combine thinly sliced beef with soy sauce, gochujang, sesame oil, minced garlic, brown sugar, and grated ginger. Let it marinate for about 15-20 minutes.

Heat vegetable oil in a skillet or wok over high heat. Add the marinated beef and cook for about 2-3 minutes until browned and cooked through. Remove from heat and set aside.

In a large pot, bring the beef broth to a simmer over medium heat.

Stir in gochujang, soy sauce, sesame oil, minced garlic, and grated ginger. Let the broth simmer for about 5 minutes to infuse the flavors.

Cook the ramen noodles according to package instructions. Drain and set aside.

Add chopped vegetables to the pot with the broth. Let them simmer for about 3-5 minutes until tender.

To serve, divide the cooked ramen noodles into serving bowls.

Ladle the hot broth and vegetables over the noodles in each bowl.

Top each bowl with a generous portion of the spicy beef.

Garnish each bowl with sliced green onions and optional toppings such as sliced boiled egg, sliced kimchi, and sesame seeds.

Serve hot and enjoy your Korean Spicy Beef Ramen!

This recipe offers a delicious fusion of Korean flavors with the comforting warmth of ramen noodles. Adjust the spice level according to your taste preference and customize the toppings to your liking. Enjoy the bold and satisfying flavors of this dish!

Sesame Ginger Ramen with Tofu

Ingredients:

For the sesame ginger sauce:

- 2 tablespoons sesame oil
- 2 tablespoons soy sauce
- 1 tablespoon rice vinegar
- 1 tablespoon grated ginger
- 2 cloves garlic, minced
- 1 teaspoon honey or maple syrup
- 1 teaspoon chili garlic sauce (optional, for extra heat)
- 1 teaspoon cornstarch (optional, for thickening)

For the ramen:

- 2 packs of ramen noodles (about 200g)
- 1 block (about 14 oz) extra-firm tofu, pressed and cubed
- 2 tablespoons vegetable oil
- 4 cups vegetable broth
- 2 cups chopped vegetables (such as bell peppers, carrots, broccoli)
- 2 green onions, thinly sliced
- Sesame seeds for garnish
- Fresh cilantro leaves for garnish
- Lime wedges for serving

Instructions:

Start by preparing the sesame ginger sauce. In a small bowl, whisk together sesame oil, soy sauce, rice vinegar, grated ginger, minced garlic, honey or maple syrup, and chili garlic sauce (if using). If you prefer a thicker sauce, you can mix in cornstarch as well. Set aside.

Cook the ramen noodles according to package instructions. Drain and set aside.

Heat vegetable oil in a large skillet or wok over medium-high heat. Add the cubed tofu and cook until golden brown on all sides, about 5-7 minutes. Remove tofu from the skillet and set aside.

In the same skillet, add chopped vegetables and stir-fry for about 3-5 minutes until they are tender-crisp.

Pour vegetable broth into the skillet and bring it to a simmer. Stir in the prepared sesame ginger sauce and let it simmer for another 2-3 minutes to thicken slightly.

Add cooked ramen noodles and tofu to the skillet. Toss everything together until the noodles and tofu are well coated with the sauce.

Divide the Sesame Ginger Ramen with Tofu into serving bowls.

Garnish each bowl with sliced green onions, sesame seeds, and fresh cilantro leaves.

Serve hot with lime wedges on the side for squeezing over the ramen.

Enjoy your flavorful and nutritious Sesame Ginger Ramen with Tofu!

This recipe offers a delicious and satisfying vegan ramen option with the rich flavors of sesame and ginger complementing the protein-packed tofu and hearty vegetables. Adjust the seasoning according to your taste preference and enjoy this comforting and nutritious dish!

Spicy Crab Ramen

Ingredients:

For the broth:

- 2 packs of ramen noodles (about 200g)
- 4 cups chicken or vegetable broth
- 1 tablespoon sesame oil
- 2 cloves garlic, minced
- 1 tablespoon grated ginger
- 2 tablespoons soy sauce
- 2 tablespoons rice vinegar
- 2 tablespoons sriracha sauce (adjust to taste)
- 1 tablespoon chili paste or sambal oelek (adjust to taste)
- Salt and pepper to taste

For the spicy crab mixture:

- 8 oz (about 225g) crab meat, fresh or canned
- 1 tablespoon mayonnaise
- 1 teaspoon sriracha sauce
- 1 teaspoon lime juice
- Salt and pepper to taste

For garnish:

- Sliced green onions
- Sesame seeds
- Lime wedges

Instructions:

In a large pot, heat sesame oil over medium heat. Add minced garlic and grated ginger, and sauté for about 1 minute until fragrant.
Pour chicken or vegetable broth into the pot and bring it to a simmer.

Stir in soy sauce, rice vinegar, sriracha sauce, and chili paste. Adjust the amount of sriracha sauce and chili paste according to your desired level of spiciness. Season with salt and pepper to taste.

Let the broth simmer for about 10-15 minutes to allow the flavors to meld. Meanwhile, prepare the spicy crab mixture. In a bowl, combine crab meat, mayonnaise, sriracha sauce, lime juice, salt, and pepper. Gently mix until well combined. Set aside.

Cook the ramen noodles according to package instructions. Drain and set aside.

To serve, divide the cooked ramen noodles into serving bowls.

Ladle the hot and spicy broth over the noodles in each bowl.

Top each bowl with a generous portion of the spicy crab mixture.

Garnish each bowl with sliced green onions, sesame seeds, and lime wedges.

Serve hot and enjoy your Spicy Crab Ramen!

This recipe offers a delightful blend of spicy broth and savory crab, all served over comforting ramen noodles. Adjust the spiciness according to your taste preference and enjoy the rich flavors of this delicious dish!

Turkey Ramen with Cranberry Sauce

Ingredients:

For the broth:

- 2 packs of ramen noodles (about 200g)
- 6 cups turkey or chicken broth
- Leftover turkey meat, shredded or chopped
- 1 onion, chopped
- 2 cloves garlic, minced
- 1 tablespoon grated ginger
- 2 carrots, sliced
- 2 celery stalks, sliced
- 1 tablespoon soy sauce
- Salt and pepper to taste

For the cranberry sauce:

- 1 cup cranberry sauce (leftover from Thanksgiving)
- 2 tablespoons soy sauce
- 1 tablespoon rice vinegar
- 1 teaspoon sesame oil
- 1 teaspoon grated ginger
- 1 teaspoon sriracha sauce (optional, for a spicy kick)

For garnish:

- Sliced green onions
- Sesame seeds
- Lime wedges

Instructions:

In a large pot, heat a bit of oil over medium heat. Add chopped onion, minced garlic, and grated ginger. Sauté until fragrant, about 2-3 minutes.

Add sliced carrots and celery to the pot and cook for another 5 minutes until slightly softened.

Pour turkey or chicken broth into the pot and bring it to a simmer.

Stir in soy sauce and season with salt and pepper to taste. Let the broth simmer for about 15-20 minutes to allow the flavors to meld.

Meanwhile, prepare the cranberry sauce. In a small saucepan, combine cranberry sauce, soy sauce, rice vinegar, sesame oil, grated ginger, and sriracha sauce (if using). Cook over low heat, stirring occasionally, until the sauce is heated through and well combined.

Cook the ramen noodles according to package instructions. Drain and set aside.

Once the broth is ready, add leftover turkey meat to the pot and let it heat through for a few minutes.

To serve, divide the cooked ramen noodles into serving bowls.

Ladle the hot turkey broth over the noodles in each bowl.

Drizzle some cranberry sauce over the turkey ramen in each bowl.

Garnish each bowl with sliced green onions, sesame seeds, and lime wedges.

Serve hot and enjoy your Turkey Ramen with Cranberry Sauce!

This recipe offers a creative and flavorful way to use up leftover Thanksgiving turkey and cranberry sauce. The combination of tender turkey, savory broth, and sweet-tart cranberry sauce creates a delicious and comforting meal. Adjust the seasoning and garnishes according to your taste preference.

Creamy Coconut Curry Ramen

Ingredients:

For the broth:

- 2 packs of ramen noodles (about 200g)
- 4 cups vegetable or chicken broth
- 1 can (14 oz) coconut milk
- 2 tablespoons red curry paste
- 2 tablespoons soy sauce
- 1 tablespoon brown sugar
- 1 tablespoon lime juice
- 2 cloves garlic, minced
- 1 tablespoon grated ginger
- 1 tablespoon vegetable oil

For the toppings:

- 1 block (about 14 oz) extra-firm tofu, pressed and cubed
- 1 red bell pepper, thinly sliced
- 1 cup sliced mushrooms (shiitake, button, or your choice)
- 2 cups baby spinach leaves
- 2 green onions, thinly sliced
- Fresh cilantro leaves for garnish
- Lime wedges for serving
- Optional: sliced chili peppers for extra heat

Instructions:

In a large pot, heat vegetable oil over medium heat. Add minced garlic and grated ginger, and cook for about 1 minute until fragrant.

Stir in red curry paste and cook for another minute to release its flavors.

Pour vegetable or chicken broth into the pot and bring it to a simmer.

Add coconut milk, soy sauce, brown sugar, and lime juice to the pot. Stir well to combine.

Let the broth simmer for about 10-15 minutes to allow the flavors to meld.

Meanwhile, prepare the toppings. In a separate skillet, heat a little oil over medium-high heat. Add cubed tofu and cook until golden brown on all sides, about 5-7 minutes. Remove tofu from the skillet and set aside.

In the same skillet, add sliced bell pepper and mushrooms. Stir-fry for about 3-5 minutes until they are tender-crisp. Add baby spinach leaves and cook for another 1-2 minutes until wilted. Remove from heat and set aside.

Cook the ramen noodles according to package instructions. Drain and set aside.

To serve, divide the cooked ramen noodles into serving bowls.

Ladle the hot coconut curry broth over the noodles in each bowl.

Top each bowl with a portion of the cooked tofu, sautéed vegetables, and sliced green onions.

Garnish each bowl with fresh cilantro leaves and serve with lime wedges on the side.

Enjoy your Creamy Coconut Curry Ramen!

This recipe offers a delicious and comforting fusion of creamy coconut curry flavors with the satisfying texture of ramen noodles. Customize the toppings according to your preferences and adjust the spice level by adding more or less red curry paste.

Buffalo Chicken Ramen

Ingredients:

For the buffalo chicken:

- 2 boneless, skinless chicken breasts, thinly sliced
- 1/4 cup hot sauce (such as Frank's RedHot)
- 2 tablespoons unsalted butter, melted
- 1 tablespoon olive oil
- Salt and pepper to taste

For the ramen:

- 2 packs of ramen noodles (about 200g)
- 4 cups chicken broth
- 2 cloves garlic, minced
- 1 tablespoon grated ginger
- 1 tablespoon soy sauce
- 1 tablespoon rice vinegar
- 1 teaspoon sesame oil
- 2 green onions, thinly sliced
- 1/4 cup crumbled blue cheese (optional)
- Celery sticks, thinly sliced (for garnish)
- Ranch dressing (for serving)

Instructions:

In a bowl, mix together hot sauce and melted butter. Season chicken breast slices with salt and pepper, then toss them in the hot sauce mixture until evenly coated.

Heat olive oil in a skillet over medium-high heat. Add the buffalo chicken slices and cook for about 4-5 minutes per side until cooked through and browned. Remove from heat and set aside.

In a large pot, bring chicken broth to a simmer over medium heat. Add minced garlic, grated ginger, soy sauce, rice vinegar, and sesame oil. Let the broth simmer for about 5 minutes to infuse the flavors.

Cook the ramen noodles according to package instructions. Drain and set aside.
To serve, divide the cooked ramen noodles into serving bowls. Ladle the hot broth over the noodles in each bowl.
Top each bowl with slices of buffalo chicken.
Garnish each bowl with sliced green onions and crumbled blue cheese (if using).
Serve hot with celery sticks on the side and a drizzle of ranch dressing over the buffalo chicken.
Enjoy your Buffalo Chicken Ramen!

This recipe offers a tasty twist on traditional ramen by incorporating the bold flavors of buffalo chicken. Adjust the level of spiciness by adding more or less hot sauce according to your preference. Feel free to customize the toppings and garnishes to suit your taste.

Printed by Libri Plureos GmbH in Hamburg, Germany